Thedralynne

The Wealth Warrior on the Trail of Money Sense

By Jennifer L Bishop

Print ISBN: 979-89862-6431-8
ebook ISBN: 979-89862-6430-1

This book is dedicated to my children Christian, Jennifer, Branden, Anisa, Alissa, Isaiah and Christina. For all the generations before you and I, to all the ones who will come after us. May the MONEY SENSE KNOWLEDGE change our lives, our community and leave a legacy of change in our mindset when it comes to thinking MONEY and WEALTH!!

My Momma always said "Act like you have some sense," and I always thought I did. Lol But we NEVER talked about MONEY SENSE KNOWLEDGE.
Well, that's because you can't teach someone something you've never taught!
That's why I want to teach you.

–Jennifer L Bishop, formerly unknowledgeable About Money Sense–

For those of us who always knew there was not enough money, but did not know how to change the situation, the knowledge of how to is here–Now!

To GOD, all the glory for giving me the words for this book. May the words help change our mindset about building wealth. Rod Watson, Christina H. Bishop and Pierre Martin for all of your technique support. To my children. Sonya Gray, helping me connect with Rod. The Leroy R. Coles, Jr branch library 1198 E. Delavan Ave Buffalo, NY 14215 thank you. Randolph Gray my illustrator, DeJaun Owens, Tim Bates, Kyrie Demby, for all your support. THANK YOU!!

This is a book about MONEY SENSE KNOWLEDGE

Table of Contents

Money Sense

The journey begins

Please allow me to introduce myself! Hello there, my name is Thedralynne (Pronounced Thed-drah-len). My friends call me Teddy, though you can choose which one you like to use! I am a Wealth Warrior (What does that mean, and why is that important to you?) and I would like to take you on a journey towards MONEY SENSE KNOWDEGLE. Now, you may be thinking, "What in the world is she talking about?" Right? I promise by the end of our journey, you will have MONEY SENSE KNOWLEDGE!

Let's Talk MONEY

Have you ever wondered how money came to be? What was life like before money? Let's start our journey here. Before paper money and coins, people would trade goods and services for goods and services as a form of payments. This is called *Bartering*. The *Bartering* system would use livestock and other large items that were considered valuable. Although valuable, these kinds of items were very inconvenient to carry around when going to do business in town. Can you imagine going to the grocery store to buy cereal and paying with chickens for the cereal? This brought the need for another way to make payments. On February 3, 1689/90 the Legislature of the Massachusetts Bay Colony issued 40,000 pounds worth of paper money, or bills of credit. The government promised the notes could be redeemed for coins. The Coinage Act of 1792- was a regulation passed by Congress on April 2, 1792, that established The United States Mint in Philadelphia. This act provided stipulations for design and production of coins. Nowadays, money comes in many different forms. We have coins, dollar bills, debit cards, credit cards and checks. The one cent is brown while all higher denominations are silver.

Paper MONEY comes in many denominations that are called *Dollar Bills*. They include the 1 Dollar Bill, 2 Dollar Bill, 5 Dollar Bill, 10 Dollar Bill, 20 Dollar Bill, 50 Dollar Bill and the 100 Dollar Bill. Is it just me or is it funny that no matter the denomination or the amount it still A Dollar Bill? Lol

Many years ago, there were high denomination Dollar Bills. There were $500 Dollar Bills, $1,000 Dollar Bills, $5,000 Dollar Bills, $10,000 Dollar Bills and even $100,000 Dollar Bills were in circulation. The $100,000 Dollar Bill was only used between financial institutions and never circulated in the general public. After the last printing of these denominations in 1945, the Treasury Department discontinued them in 1969. Here are a few photos.

But money comes in different forms. Checks are a form of *money.* They are issued by the *bank,* which also may issue the *bank's Debit Card* when you open a checking account. These cards are convenient and easy to carry instead of cash *money* and have a set amount of money that they are worth and can be used for. Take a look at the *Debit* cards pictured here.

Notice the *Visa logo* and on the right lower corner of each card with the word *DEBIT* above the visa logo. These cards pictured here show you how *Debit* looks. The *debit* card is directly connected to a *bank account.*

These cards pictured below are *CREDIT* Cards. Notice there is only the *Visa* or *Mastercard* logo on these cards. The word *DEBIT* does NOT appear on these cards.

People use different names for MONEY, but they all means the same thing MONEY.

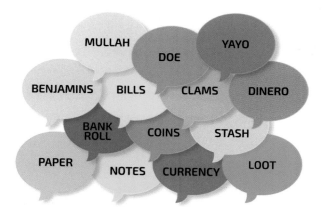

Checks are issued by the *BANK* when you open a checking account. They are convenient to have instead of carrying cash *money,* and checks spend just like cash *money.*

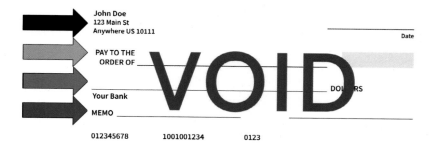

➡ Your Name, address and phone number will be in the upper left corner of the *CHECK* and the date on the right side.

➡ Pay to the order of, this is who you are writing the *check* out to, to pay.

➡ The dollar amount is written out on this line for payment.

➡ This space is for a memo about the payment, the right corner space is for your signature.

Here is how *CHECKS* work. When you open a checking account, you have to put *money* into the account. When You do this, you are making a *DEPOSIT*. The amount you deposit into the account is the amount you can use when writing your checks at different stores and businesses. It is very important that you keep track of the money you put in your *BANK ACCOUNT* and the amount you spend when writing your *CHECKS* or *using your DEBIT CARD*.

NEVER WRITE CHECKS WHEN YOU DO NOT HAVE THE MONEY IN YOUR ACCOUNT OR WRITE CHECKS FOR MORE MONEY THAN YOU HAVE IN YOUR ACCOUNT!!

If you do, this is called an *OVERDRAFT* and you will have to pay an *INSUFFICIENT* funds fee, which is a charge the bank adds to your account for not having money. If this happens on a regular basis this is very expensive, and the bank may even close your account. The *DEBIT* card is used in place of cash money and is directly connected to your bank account. When you use it, the money is taken out of your bank account immediately. It is very important to keep a daily record when writing *CHECKS* and using your *DEBIT CARDS* so you do not spend more than you have in your *BANK ACCOUNT*, and so that you know when to *deposit* more *MONEY* into your account.

DEBIT cards and *CREDIT* cards are sometimes referred to as plastic money because the cards are square, small in size and made of plastic. The cards look alike, but remember the *DEBIT CARD* will have the word *DEBIT* on it and the *CREDIT* card will not. And although they look alike, they work differently.

The *CREDIT CARD* is used in place of cash money to buy all kinds of goods and services we need daily. It is *CREDIT* that is being extended to the person whose name is one the cars. What does this mean? A person gets to use someone else's money to buy goods and services.

It is like borrowing: They buy now and pay later. This is *CREDIT* (sometimes there is a *fee* when we pay later) It is a very special privilege and should not be taken for granted.

Why do we need *CREDIT*? There will be times in life when you will need to purchase things that will cost more than you have cash *MONEY* to buy. Like when you buy a home or even a car.

This is when you will need *CREDIT*. To get a *CREDIT* card, you will fill out an application for *CREDIT* with the bank or business where you want *CREDIT*. (See Consumer Credit Application)

CONSUMER CREDIT APPLICATION

Name/Address

Name				Social Security Number	
Address:					
City:	State/Province:	ZIP/Postal code:	Phone:		Work:
Own Rent (Please circle) Monthly payment or rent		How long?			
Previous Address:					
City:	State/Province:	ZIP/Postal code:	Phone:		Work:
Owned Rented (Please circle) Monthly payment or rent		How long?			

Employment History

Employer 1:			Job Title:	
Address:			Supervisor:	
City:	State/Province:	ZIP/Postal code:	Salary:	
Phone:		Date From:	Date To:	
Employer 2:			Job Title:	
Address:			Supervisor:	
City:	State/Province:	ZIP/Postal code:	Salary:	
Phone:		Date From:	Date To:	

Source of Income	Total	Expenses	Total
Salary		Loans	
Bonuses & Commissions		Charge Account bills	
Income from Rental Property		Monthly Bills	
Investment Income		Real Estate Mortgages	
Other Income		Other Debts -- Itemize	
Total Income		**Total Expenses**	

Bank References

Institution Name:	Institution Name:	Institution Name:	
Checking Account #	Savings Account #	Loan #	Loan Balance:
Address:	Address:	Address:	
Contact/Phone:	Contact/Phone:	Contact/Phone:	

Credit Cards

Type:	Account No.	Current Balance
Type:	Account No.	Current Balance
Type:	Account No.	Current Balance

Bankruptcy

Have you gone bankrupt in the last five years?   ( ) Yes ( ) No / If yes, give date of assignment:

I hereby certify that the information contained herein is complete and accurate. This information has been furnished with the understanding that it is to be used to determine the amount and conditions of the credit to be extended. Furthermore, I hereby authorize the financial institutions listed in this credit application to release necessary information to the company for which credit is being applied for to verify the information contained herein.

_____   _____
Signature   Date

One the *CREDIT* card application, you will answer questions about yourself, such as where you work, how much you earn yearly, how long you have worked there. You will also be asked where you live and how long you have lived there. You will need references, either business or personal ones.

References are people or businesses that will say you are a person who keeps his or her word and pays their bills. All of this information is important when trying to get a *CREDIT* card.

The "Who" in Who Needs MONEY

Do you ever stop and think about it? It? What it? MONEY. No! You don't think about it; we don't think about it. We never really think about MONEY. No! You do not, we do not. We just think about what I want or need. Never really thinking about the MONEY or rather the connection between the need and wants that go along with the MONEY.

So let's stop and think about the "who" in who needs MONEY? Here we go. EVERYONE needs MONEY for everything. Wow! Now that you are thinking about, that says a lot, oh my. If you could step in front of a mirror and take a look at your reflection, You could see from the top of your head to the bottom of your feet MONEY. Now you might be thinking what is Teddy talking about? Here's what I'm talking about. Whether you're a boy or a girl, you have to take care of your hair. Haircuts, washing, conditioning and styling.

MONEY. But you may not think it that way. You probably say, "Mom or Dad, I need a haircut" or "Mom I need to go to the hairdresser." But it is still MONEY. Not from your pockets, unless you have a job, or get allowance. These things are taken care of by our parents. All we think about when it comes to MONEY is 'I need." And that beautiful skin your body is wrapped in? Well, we have to clean our bodies and moisturize it! Remember cleanliness is good for you as well as everyone around you. No ashy knees or elbows here. YES! MONEY! A place to live? Everyone needs a home. If you're buying it, you pay the mortgage until it's paid in full. If you're not, then you pay rent monthly. Either way, it's MONEY. But we can't just have a building. We need heat in the winter and air conditioning in the summer, and lights so we can see when the sun goes down. We need electricity. MONEY!

House: MONEY

Lights: MONEY

Hot Water: MONEY

Food: MONEY

Furniture: MONEY

Water: MONEY

All these things are needed daily in our homes. Did you see that car drive by? Yes, MONEY

13

Car: MONEY

Tires: MONEY Gas: MONEY

Car Insurance MONEY

To be blessed with having a car to drive, you will probably pay a car note monthly. A car is an expensive purchase, and most people do not have the cash MONEY to pay for it in full. Instead, they borrow the money from the bank and then you pay the bank back monthly. This is called a *Car* note. But that's still not it! You need car insurance to keep you and others safe when you drive to work, MONEY! Oh yeah, then there's the gas so you can drive to work and anywhere else you want to go. So just looking in the mirror or looking out of the window at a home, you can see that MONEY is needed everywhere by everyone. The point I want to make is that every person, no matter how young or old they are, they all need MONEY to live daily. So! The "Who" in "Who needs MONEY" is YOU, ME and EVERYBODY!!!!!!!!

Why You Need MONEY

Everything in life is connected to a cost. Our basic needs like food, water and shelter all cost. When you are hungry and need to eat, your parents have to buy food to feed you. They have to cook your meal in a home on the stove. The home, the food, and the energy needed to cook the food are all associated with a cost. In our daily walk, through life, there is a cost associated with living. Everywhere! You look around, and you will see the various ways money is needed.

Without money, life would be very difficult. You would not have food to eat or be able to take care of yourself if there were no way to pay for these basic things. So now you know: Everyone needs the use of MONEY to live. Children don't have money. But your parents do, and when you need food, clothes, toys, school supplies or even pet food, Moms and Dads, Grandparents, Aunties and Uncles spend the money they earn from working a job to take care of your needs. The money they earn is called an *income*.

Let us look back over what we have learned about money so far:

We need MONEY to buy the things we need to live every day.

MONEY can be called many different names, but they all mean the same MONEY!

We Need MONEY to live! Everywhere we look, we see how we need MONEY in everyday life. Most people earn MONEY by working a job.

When you have a job, you earn a paycheck. The paycheck is an *income* and this is what we spend to live.

How Does MONEY Work

To get the MONEY we all need to live daily, we have to have a source. An *income* is a great source. An income is what a job pays you. Here's an example of how we earn:

You get hired at Bev's Bakery for $15 an hour. You work five days a week, working six hours a day. That's 30 hours a week. Your weekly income is calculated like this:

$15 a hour x six hours a day = $90 a day that you would earn.

$ 90 a day x five days = $ 450 weekly.

$ 450 a week x four weeks = $ 1,800 monthly.

$ 1,800 a month X 12 monthly = 21,600 yearly. This is an example of how to earn a yearly *income*.

There are other variables in the real world that I did not use in this example. *Gross income* is what you earn before *taxes* are taken out; and *net income* is earned after taxes are taken out, ok? I just want you to get the basic idea of *income*.

(*Taxes:* When you work and get paid, the government takes a small part of your paycheck to pay for things like schools and playgrounds that everybody can use. The money that the government takes for these purposes is called a tax.)

We know everything is connected to a cost in life, so people need jobs to earn *income,* and they need MONEY to survive.

Now that we know about MONEY, how it looks, who needs it (everyone!) and how we earn it, let's get to how it works for us in the real world! You know how our parents want us to do well in school and get good grades so we can get a good report card?

Report Card	
Math	A+
History	B
Spelling	A+
Science	B
English	A+

We do that so that we can get promoted to the next grade each year until we graduate from Elementary, Middle, High School and even College. Getting good grades is very important to keep you moving forward so that you will be promoted to the next grade all the way through school. We get all the education we can in order to be successful when we grow up, and go out into the world to get a good job so we can earn an income. We do that so that we can have a home and all the things we need daily. When you are all grown up and start working to earn an income, paying your bills and borrowing MONEY, you get a report card on how you pay your bills and pay back the MONEY borrowed, either by getting a loan or by using your credit cards.

Wow, grownups get a report card too! Yes, they get a FICO Score (a report card for adults). Everything that we have been learning on the MONEY Sense Trail has been very important! What you are going to learn next is EXTREMELY important, so pay close attention! In school, after you have been taught lessons, you take a test to see how well you have learned the lessons. When you are taking the test, there are teachers to watch over the class as you take the test. Let's call them test monitors.

Well, in adult life, there are monitors also. The report card you get as a grownup is called a FICO Score. Bill Fair and Earl Isaac created it in 1956. Notice the "F" is from Fair, the "I" is from Isaac and the "CO" is from Company--this is how we get to FICO. There are three FICO monitors. We will call them Ms. Experian, Mr. Equifax and Mr. Transunion, and they will monitor how good you are at paying back money you borrowed. They also monitor how much you have borrowed and how good you are at paying your bills on time. This is considered a measure of consumer risk (you are the consumer, a person who purchases goods and services for personal use).

Credit is an agreement (contract) that can be based on your word or a written contract. The *borrower* is the person getting something now and paying for it later. The *lender* is a business or person that provides the MONEY and says, "OK, you can pay me back later." When you pay later, there is sometimes a cost, and the cost is called *interest*. Business and Banks extend *credit* to the *borrower*, and the borrower pays *interest* for using the *credit*, plus the original amount that was borrowed, which is called the *principal*. Now, you may be wondering how all these things work together in life, right? Let us look at a few examples of when and how *credit* can be used in life.

William and Isaiah are 4th graders and have been best friends since kindergarten. This year they are in the same classroom! They get to eat lunch together, and this is great because they sometimes swap their lunch items. Today William has homemade Rice Krispy treats and Isaiah doesn't have anything that William wants to trade for. Isaiah sees that there is enough to share. And, so he asks William,

"If you give me half of your Rice Krispy treat, I'll pay you 50 cents tomorrow." William considers the fact that they are best friends and he trusts Isaiah. Isaiah gave his word, and this is a verbal contract: He's getting something today and paying for it later based on his word! (If Isaiah was an adult and borrowed M O N E Y, he would be using *Credit* and this would be reported on his FICO Score)

Let's look at another example:

Alissa has just graduated from Spelman College with a bachelor's degree in business finance. She has a job offer from Volkswagen in Nashville, Tenn., as a financial analyst. She is very excited and nervous at the same time. She will need to find a place to live and furnish her new home. Alissa does not have a lot of M O N E Y, because she's a college graduate just starting out. She has found an apartment and filled out the application for residency, where they require a deposit because her FICO Score (her adult report card) is so new that it has no grade on it. But she was approved for the apartment. She still needs furniture and decides to apply for a *Credit* card at Nash Co Furniture & Mattress. Again, Alissa's FICO Score (her adult report card) is so new that there is no information on her history of paying bills on time or paying back M O N E Y that she has borrowed or paid off her *Credit* cards. But she gets approved for $1,200. That's not enough for everything for her apartment, so she will just get a bedroom set and a washer and dryer. Nash Co Furniture & Mattress tells Alissa if she makes all her payments over the next six month's they will increase her limit so that she can buy items.

This makes Aliss very happy! Her payments are $150 plus $18 in *interest,* for a total of $168 monthly.

How does this example relate to your adult report card, your FICO Score (report Card)? you keep your word and make your payments on time, every time, you get an "A"!

This is excellent and means you will have more options when *borrowing* MONEY or getting *Credit* your interest *rate* will be very low or possibly even 0%. The lower you rate, the less MONEY you will have to pay in interest. Your, FICO Score (or grade) will need to be between 850 and 720

A "B" FICO Score (or grade) is good, and is between 719 and 690. In this case, you might have paid late, but you got caught up. Still, it drops the grade. Your *interest* rate will be low but not as low as it would be if you had an "A" FICO Score. "B" is good, but *not* the best.

A "C" FICO Score is *fair,* and between 689 and 630. This means you have had more than one late payment and your credit cards are maxed out, meaning you've used up all the credit that companies have given you. Your *interest rate* here is very high so you are paying more than if your FICO Score (grade) was a "A" or a "B".

A "D" FICO Score is 629 and lower. THIS IS VERY, VERY, BAD AND YOU DO NOT EVER WANT TO BE HERE!!! IF YOU ARE HERE, YOU MAY NOT BE ABLE TO GET THE LOAN OR CREDIT, AND IF YOU DO GET THEM. YOU ARE PAYING THE HIGHEST INTEREST RATE ALLOWED!!!

```
┌─────────────────────────────┐
│         FICO Score          │
│        Report Card          │
│                             │
│   850-720    Excellent  A   │
│                             │
│   719-690    Good       B   │
│                             │
│   689-630    Fair       C   │
│                             │
│   629 & Below  Poor     D   │
│                             │
└─────────────────────────────┘
```

Remember When I told you there would be times in life when you would need more MONEY than you have for things in life? Well, this is how it all works together. When you need a home or car or other expensive purchases, you will have to borrow the money from the *bank* or get *credit* from a business. The *bank* or *business* will send information to the monitors-- you remember Ms. Experian, Mr. Equifax and Mr. Transunion-- about how well you are keeping your word and making on-time payments. They then calculate your FICO Score (report card) and whenever you need to *borrow* money or take out *credit,* the banks and business go to the monitors and ask how well you are keeping your word. Keeping your word is EXTREMELY IMPORTANT because this will determine how much you can borrow and how low or high the *interest rate* will be when you pay for using the money or credit to buy now and paying later, it can also play a part where you live. So, remember, your FICO Score (report card) is more than important! It will determine where you live and how you will be able to get *credit* or *borrow* money throughout your adult life to buy the things you want and need! Make well thought of decisions before purchasing things.

Our journey on the Money Sense Trail is quickly to the end, but before I say goodbye let's take a review on what we have learned!

Everyone needs MONEY, no matter their age, young or older we need MONEY each and every day.

We all need MONEY, everything that goes along with living!! Life would be IMPOSSIBLE to live without MONEY.

Money is monumental to how we live OUR lives.

Once you understand how it works in life, you will be equipped to make well informed decisions concerning MONEY.

Knowing that you will be given a FICO Score your entire adult life and understanding how it works is key to your success.

Always, remember to keep your word, pay your bills on time every time, this will affect if you pay NO or very low interest rates when borrowing money.

That means you want to have an A FICO Score, if possible, although B FICO Score is ok but C is really not the best. D not the greatest at all if you get the approval, you will be paying the highest interest allowed.

We, Wealth Warriors, know you know how to travel along the Money sense Trail with confidence. Remember the rules and make the best decisions for your life. Always remember you are in control of how and when you spend your MONEY, spend it wisely and MONEY will take care of you.

GLOSSARY

Bank: A financial institution that accepts deposits from the public.

Bank Account: An arrangement made with a bank whereby one may deposit and withdraw money and in some cases be paid interest.

Bartering: The action or system of exchanging goods or services without using money. Borrowing: The action of borrowing something.

Car Insurance: Insurance against loss from destruction of or damage to an insured motorist vehicle.

Checking Account: a bank account from which money can be easily transferred. Coin: A flat, typical round piece of metal with an official stamp, used as money

Credit Card: A small plastic card issued by a bank, business, ect, allowing the holder to Purchase goods or services on credit.

Debit Card: A card issued by a bank allowing the holder to transfer money electronically to another bank account when making a purchase.

Deposit: A sum of money placed or kept in a bank account, usually to gain interest.

Federal Reserve System: The federal reserve system is the central banking system of the United States of America. It was created on December 23, 1913

Gross Income: Is an individual's total earnings before taxes.

Line of Credit: A credit facility extended by a Bank or other financial institution to a government, business or individual customer that enables the customer to draw on the facility when the customer needs funds.

Insufficient Funds: An insufficient funds fee (sometimes referred to as an non-sufficient funds Fee or NSF) can occur when you don't have enough money in your checking account to cover the *entire* transaction.

Interest Rates: The portion of a loan that is charged as interest to the borrower, typically expressed as an annual percentage of the loan outstanding.

Overdraft: A deficit in a bank account caused by drawing more money than the account holds.

Net Income: The balance of Gross Income remaining after all allowable deductions and exemptions are taken.

Paper Checks: As a negotiable payment instrument in the United States. Plastic Money: Credit cards, used instead of cash.

Treasury Department: The government department that is in charge of handling a country's money.

References

Investopedia.com

Dictionary.com

Wikipedia.com

Google.com

Merriam Webster